Death

by Helen Orme

Trailblazers

Death

by Helen Orme

Illustrated by Martin Bolchover

Published by Ransom Publishing Ltd.
51 Southgate Street, Winchester, Hampshire SO23 9EH
www.ransom.co.uk

ISBN 978 184167 591 6

First published in 2006
Second printing 2007

A CIP catalogue record of this book is available from the British Library.

Death

Contents

Get the facts **5**

Why do people die? 6

How do you know if someone is dead? 8

What happens to the body? 10

Funerals 12

Memorials 14

All Soul's Day 16

Fiction

Not my Fault 19

Death word check **36**

Death

Get the facts

Why do people die?

All living things die.

Most people die when they are very old. Their bodies wear out and stop working properly.

People die because they do not have enough food to eat.

People die in accidents.

This might be an accident at work, at home or in a car.

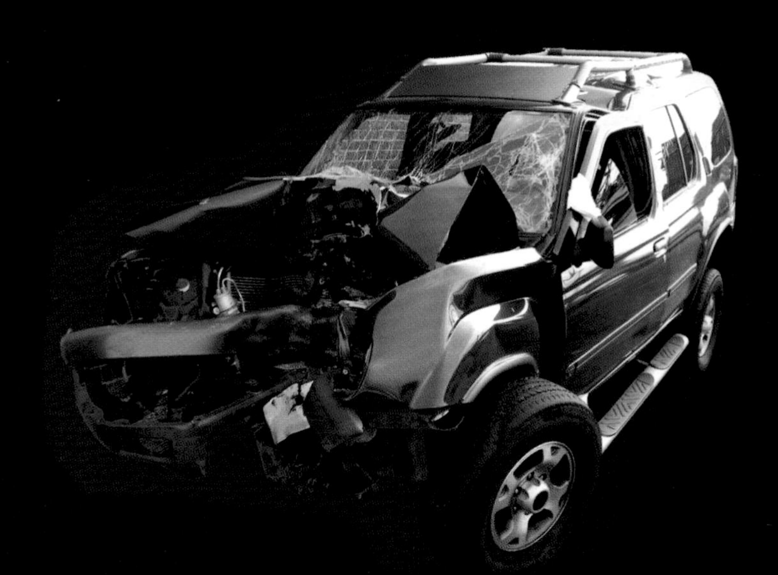

This table shows deaths in road accidents for the year 2000.

Age groups	5 - 14	15 - 24	25 - 34	35 - 44	45 - 54	Totals
Males	83	578	528	356	212	2331
Females	43	159	95	82	82	867

- Which age group has the most deaths?
- Why do you think this is?
- Why do you think more boys have died than girls?

How do you know someone is dead?

A person is dead if:

- They have stopped breathing.
- Their heart has stopped beating.
- Their brain has stopped working.

What do you do when someone dies?

A doctor gives you a death certificate. This tells you why the person died.

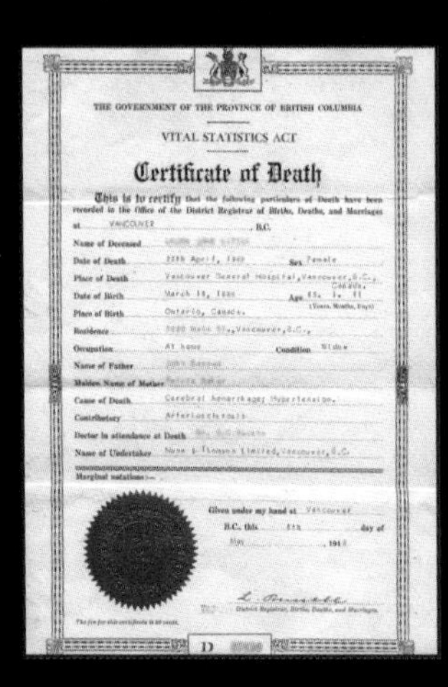

THE GOVERNMENT OF THE PROVINCE OF BRITISH COLUMBIA

VITAL STATISTICS ACT

Certificate of Death

This is to certify that the following particulars of Death have been recorded in the Office of the District Registrar of Births, Deaths, and Marriages at Vancouver, B.C.

Name of Deceased

Date of Death | Sex Female

Place of Death Vancouver General Hospital, Vancouver, B.C., Canada.

Date of Birth | Age (Years, Months, Days)

Place of Birth Ontario, Canada.

Residence

Occupation At home | Condition Widow

Name of Father

Maiden Name of Mother

Cause of Death

Contributory

Doctor in attendance at Death

Name of Undertaker

Marginal notations:—

Given under my hand at Vancouver B.C. this day of May, 19

District Registrar, Births, Deaths, and Marriages.

D

You take the certificate to a registry office where they record details about the dead person.

People use death certificates to help them find out about their family history.

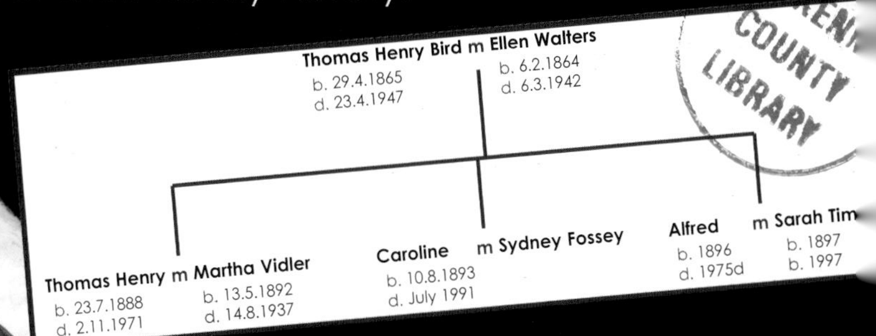

When someone dies in an accident the police are called. There will be an inquest.

People in the accident, or people who saw it, have to give evidence. This helps the police decide who was to blame.

What happens to the body?

In most countries dead bodies are buried or cremated (burnt).

In northern Canada, people who die in the winter cannot be buried straight away. The bodies are kept, until the ground warms up and graves can be dug.

Hindus believe that bodies should be burnt.

Very religious Hindus want their ashes to be put in the River Ganges.

In Tibet bodies are given a sky burial.

Bodies are put outside and left for birds to eat the flesh.

In other places, bodies are left in towers or trees.

On one South Sea Island bodies were left on the reefs for sharks to eat. (This was a long time ago.)

Funerals

When someone dies their family and friends have a funeral.

This shows respect for the dead person. It is a good way to help people feel better when someone they love has died.

Another way of showing how you feel is to leave flowers.

People send flowers to be put on a grave.

Some people like to put stones to show where a grave is.

If someone has died in an accident, people leave flowers near where they were killed.

Sometimes the name of the dead person is written in a special book.

Memorials

In the past important people, like kings, built special tombs for themselves and their families.

The Taj Mahal was built by an Indian king to show how much he loved his wife.

Egyptian kings (Pharaohs) built wonderful tombs under the ground. They filled their tombs with things that the king had used while he was alive.

In China, this king had models of his soldiers, made of clay, buried with him.

All Soul's Day

All Soul's Day is November 2. It is also called the 'Day of the Dead'.

It is an important festival in some countries, especially Mexico.

People believed that the dead would come home for a meal with their family on that day.

Now the festival is just for fun.

People like to dress up.

The shops sell cakes and sweets made to look like skulls or skeletons.

They make special round loaves of bread called 'pan de muertos' ('bread of the dead'). These loaves are decorated with candy 'bones' or sugar skulls.

Trail Blazers

Not my Fault

Chapter 1:
Late again

Sally was tired. She was fed up. Mum was always late.

She looked up as the gang left.

"Wanna lift?"

She smiled at Charlie and shook her head.

"Mum will be here soon."

Charlie grinned.

"Yeah! About three hours late if I know your mum."

"Come on Charlie," called Simon. He was grinning stupidly. Sally glared. He was drunk again.

She really liked Charlie but she didn't much like the rest of them.

Come on, Charlie!
Your mum's late. Want a lift, Sally?
No thanks. She'll be here soon.

It was ages before mum got there.

"Sorry, sorry, sorry," said mum.

"You said ten o'clock." said Sally. "It's nearly eleven – everyone has gone."

Sally got into the car and fell asleep.

She woke, suddenly, to the sound of sirens. Blue lights flashed. An ambulance roared past, then another, then a police car.

"Bother," said mum. "There must have been an accident on the hill. I'll have to go the long way home."

Sorry I was late, Sally.
She's always late.
Looks like there's been an accident. We'll have to go the long way home.

Chapter 2: Bad news

Next day, at college, she heard the news.

Charlie had smashed the car. He had a broken leg and had hurt his head. He'd had an operation. He was O.K., but he just wouldn't wake up.

Everyone at college was talking about the accident.

"Charlie's a killer!" said Julie.

Next day at college, there is bad news.
Charlie's a KILLER!
The Herald
3 DIE IN CAR SMASH

Julie had been Simon's girlfriend and now Simon was dead.

All the others in the car had died: Simon, Craig and Craig's girlfriend Rachel.

Everyone blamed Charlie.

"He was drunk," they said.

It wasn't true! Sally knew it wasn't true.

But Charlie couldn't explain. He was still asleep.

It was Charlie's fault. He was driving and he was DRUNK!
But it's not true . . .
The Herald
3 DIE IN CAR SMASH
Charlie was still asleep in hospital . . .

Chapter 3:
Not Charlie

Sally's mum was driving her to college.

They passed the place where Charlie had gone off the road.

The police had put tapes round, to keep people away.

The first day the car had still been there. It was horrible. The front was bashed in. But the side was worse. It had been ripped right off.

People went to look. They came back to college and told everyone about it.

"There was loads of blood everywhere!"

"You could see the marks where they put the bodies!"

Sally hated it.

Sally's mum was driving her to college. Past the place where the accident had happened . . .
I hate coming past here.

Other people had left flowers along the roadside. They left letters and poems and photos.

Sally wanted to go and leave some flowers, but her mum wouldn't take her.

She kept on and on about Charlie.

"It was all his fault."

But Sally knew she was wrong.

People had left flowers at the scene . . .
You're wrong!
It was Charlie's fault!

Chapter 4: Whose fault?

Good news. Charlie had woken up. But he couldn't remember anything about the accident.

The police gave their evidence in court.

There was no alcohol in Charlie's blood. He hadn't been drinking.

Then there was a real shock.

The police said there had been another car. Charlie wasn't speeding. They had proved that. A large car had rounded the bend, too fast, too far across the road.

Charlie had swerved but the road had been wet. He hadn't had a chance.

The police put up notices. They wanted to talk to anyone who had been driving that way when the accident happened.

Charlie had woken up, but he didn't remember what had happened.
The driver WASN'T drunk. Another car caused the accident by going too fast.
ACCIDENT
DO YOU HAVE INFORMATION?
RING THE POLIC

Sally remembered something.

"Why haven't you been to the police?" she asked her mum. "You were there."

Her mum just looked at her.

"Soon," she said "Soon."

And she started to cry.

Then Sally understood.

She knew exactly what had happened.

Mum had been late. She was always late.

And when she was late she drove too fast!

Why haven't you been to the police? You were there!
Soon. I'll go soon.
Mum was late. And when she's late she drives TOO FAST . . . !!

Death word check

accident

alcohol

All Souls Day

ambulance

breathing

cremated

college

death certificate

evidence

family tree

festival

flowers

funeral

Hindus

inquest

record

registry office

skeleton

skull

speeding

stupidly

swerved

tomb